TAMPA BAY
BUCCANEERS

BY TODD KORTEMEIER

SportsZone
An Imprint of Abdo Publishing
abdopublishing.com

abdopublishing.com

Published by Abdo Publishing, a division of ABDO, PO Box 398166, Minneapolis, Minnesota 55439. Copyright © 2017 by Abdo Consulting Group, Inc. International copyrights reserved in all countries. No part of this book may be reproduced in any form without written permission from the publisher. SportsZone™ is a trademark and logo of Abdo Publishing.

Printed in the United States of America, North Mankato, Minnesota
042016
092016

THIS BOOK CONTAINS RECYCLED MATERIALS

Cover Photo: Brian Blanco/AP Images
Interior Photos: Brian Blanco/AP Images, 1; Al Golub/AP Images, 4-5; Allen Kee/AP Images, 6, 7; Arthur Anderson/AP Images, 8-9; Al Messerschmidt/AP Images, 10, 11, 12-13, 14-15, 20-21, 22, 23; Vernon Biever/AP Images, 16; Thom Baur/AP Images, 17; Greg Trott/AP Images, 18-19; Newman Lorance/NFL Photos/AP Images, 24-25; Denis Poroy/AP Images, 26-27; Aaron M. Sprecher/AP Images, 28-29

Editor: Patrick Donnelly
Series Designer: Nikki Farinella

Cataloging-in-Publication Data
Names: Kortemeier, Todd, author.
Title: Tampa Bay Buccaneers / by Todd Kortemeier.
Description: Minneapolis, MN : Abdo Publishing, [2017] | Series: NFL up close | Includes index.
Identifiers: LCCN 2015960456 | ISBN 9781680782356 (lib. bdg.) |
    ISBN 9781680776461 (ebook)
Subjects: LCSH: Tampa Bay Buccaneers (Football team)--History--Juvenile literature. | National Football League--Juvenile literature. | Football--Juvenile literature. | Professional sports--Juvenile literature. | Football teams--Florida--Juvenile literature.
Classification: DDC 796.332--dc23
LC record available at http://lccn.loc.gov/2015960456

TABLE OF CONTENTS

FINALLY CHAMPIONS 4

GROWING PAINS 8

FIRST SUCCESS 12

LEAN YEARS 16

GOLDEN ERA 20

GRUDEN AND BEYOND 24

Timeline 30
Glossary 31
Index / About the Author 32

FINALLY CHAMPIONS

It could have been called the Pirate Bowl. The Tampa Bay Buccaneers faced the Oakland Raiders in the Super Bowl. The Bucs had the league's best defense in the 2002 season. The Raiders had the best offense. Something had to give.

FAST FACT
Buccaneers coach Jon Gruden faced his old team in this Super Bowl. He coached the Raiders from 1998 to 2001.

Jon Gruden was just 39 years old when he coached the Buccaneers to the Super Bowl.

Tampa Bay's defense, led by linebacker Derrick Brooks and safety John Lynch, won the day. Oakland's quarterback Rich Gannon was the league's Most Valuable Player (MVP). But Gannon threw five interceptions that day. The Buccaneers returned three of them for touchdowns. Tampa Bay routed the Raiders 48-21.

It was more than the defining moment of a great season. It erased 26 years of frustration. The Tampa Bay Buccaneers had finally become champions.

Dexter Jackson races toward the end zone with one of his two interceptions in the Super Bowl.

FAST FACT

With two interceptions, Bucs safety Dexter Jackson was named Super Bowl MVP. He was just the third defensive back to win that award.

Bucs defensive end Simeon Rice and his teammates made life miserable for Oakland quarterback Rich Gannon.

The Buccaneers and quarterback Steve Spurrier were no match for the giants of the NFL in their first season.

GROWING PAINS

The Buccaneers joined the National Football League (NFL) in 1976. They came into the league as an expansion team. Their players were all rookies or guys who the other teams did not want. This team of castoffs was short on both talent and experience. The young Buccaneers struggled to compete.

FAST FACT

The Buccaneers' first quarterback was Steve Spurrier. He went on to become a national championship-winning coach in college football.

The Buccaneers did not score a touchdown until their fourth game. They averaged just 8.9 points per game. Only three other NFL teams have ever done worse than that. But the most important number of the season was zero. That was the number of games they won. With a 31-14 loss to the New England Patriots on December 12, the Bucs finished the 1976 season 0-14.

The losses kept piling up. Tampa Bay lost its first 12 games of the next season before finally winning their first game on December 11, 1977, against the New Orleans Saints. But in 1978, the team drafted quarterback Doug Williams. He would help lead the Bucs out of the NFL's basement.

Tampa Stadium

FAST FACT

The Buccaneers' first home was Tampa Stadium. It was nicknamed "The Big Sombrero" because its shape was similar to the famous Mexican hat.

Strong-armed quarterback Doug Williams helped turn the Buccaneers into winners.

11

FIRST SUCCESS

The 1976 season was one to forget for the Buccaneers and their fans. But they found some solid players along the way. Fifteen players from the 1976 team were still with the Bucs in 1979. That is when they finally broke through.

Doug Williams pitches the ball to running back Ricky Bell, *42*, in a 1979 game at Tampa Stadium.

FAST FACT

John McKay coached the Buccaneers for their first nine seasons. McKay had coached the Southern California Trojans to four college national championships.

The NFL's top-ranked defense led the Buccaneers to a 10-6 record and a division championship. Defensive end Lee Roy Selmon was named the NFL Defensive Player of the Year. The Bucs beat the Philadelphia Eagles in their first playoff game. That brought them just one game away from the Super Bowl. But they fell short. They lost to the Los Angeles Rams 9-0.

After a down year in 1980, the Bucs returned to the playoffs in the next two seasons. But they still fell short of the Super Bowl.

Lee Roy Selmon was a defensive force for the Buccaneers in the late 1970s.

FAST FACT

Doug Williams left Tampa Bay after the 1982 season. Five years later he led Washington to a Super Bowl title. He was the first black quarterback to win a Super Bowl.

LEAN YEARS

The 1982 playoff appearance was the last one for quite a while. From 1983 through 1996, the Bucs did not even get close to a winning record. They had some good players, such as quarterback Vinny Testaverde and running back James Wilder. But they could not put together a winner.

James Wilder fights through the mud in a 1984 game against the Green Bay Packers.

Vinny Testaverde was the Buccaneers' starting quarterback for five and a half seasons.

FAST FACT
Through 2015, James Wilder is still the Bucs' all-time leader with 5,957 rushing yards.

Trent Dilfer throws a pass against the San Francisco 49ers in a 1994 game.

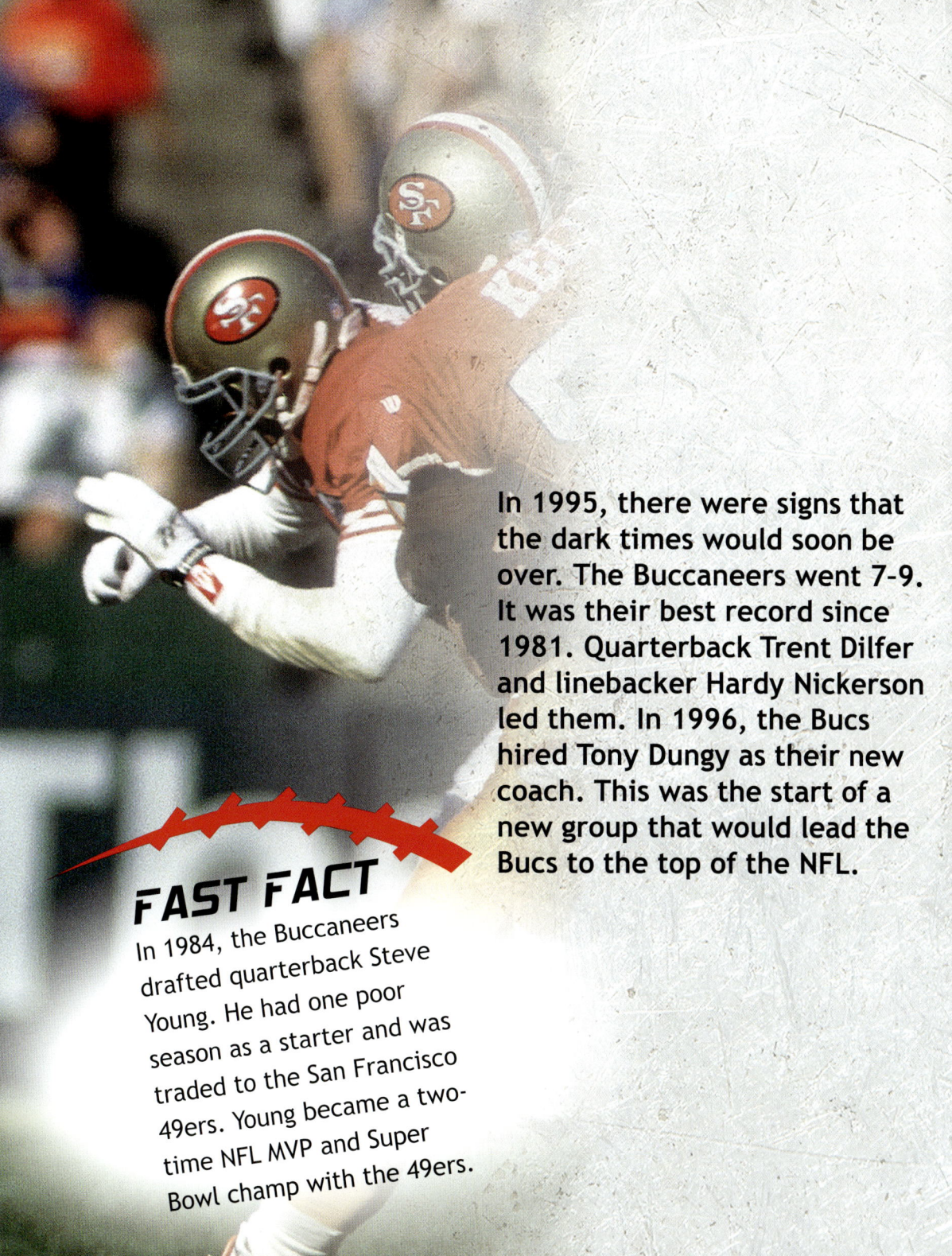

In 1995, there were signs that the dark times would soon be over. The Buccaneers went 7-9. It was their best record since 1981. Quarterback Trent Dilfer and linebacker Hardy Nickerson led them. In 1996, the Bucs hired Tony Dungy as their new coach. This was the start of a new group that would lead the Bucs to the top of the NFL.

FAST FACT

In 1984, the Buccaneers drafted quarterback Steve Young. He had one poor season as a starter and was traded to the San Francisco 49ers. Young became a two-time NFL MVP and Super Bowl champ with the 49ers.

GOLDEN ERA

When Tony Dungy took over in 1996, he improved the Buccaneers' defense immediately. They went from being ranked 27th in yards allowed to 11th. The next year, they improved to third in the NFL. The Bucs went 10-6 and made the playoffs. They remained in the top 10 in defense for the rest of Dungy's time in Tampa Bay.

FAST FACT

In 1997, the Bucs changed their logo and uniforms. They went from orange and white to red and pewter with a new logo. These uniforms remained basically unchanged until 2014.

Tony Dungy talks to reporters in front of the Buccaneers' new logo.

Tampa Bay had excellent defensive players during this time. Linebacker Derrick Brooks made all the plays. Big Warren Sapp plugged the middle of the line and sacked the quarterback. They also had a powerful rushing attack with Mike Alstott and Warrick Dunn.

The Bucs made the playoffs four times under Dungy. They even reached the conference championship game after the 1999 season. But the St. Louis Rams came back to win in the final minutes. Tampa Bay's first Super Bowl would have to wait.

Mike Alstott punished NFL defenses with his bruising running style.

Warrick Dunn was a quick, elusive running back whose sharp cuts often left defenders grasping at air.

FAST FACT

In 1998, the Bucs moved into Raymond James Stadium in Tampa. Its most notable feature is a 103-foot (31.4-m) long pirate ship behind the north end zone.

23

Warren Sapp stuffs Chicago Bears running back James Allen in a 2000 game.

GRUDEN AND BEYOND

While Tony Dungy transformed the Buccaneers' fortunes, he could not lead them to a championship. In 2002, they turned to coach Jon Gruden. The move paid off right away. Tampa Bay built the league's best defense and won the Super Bowl.

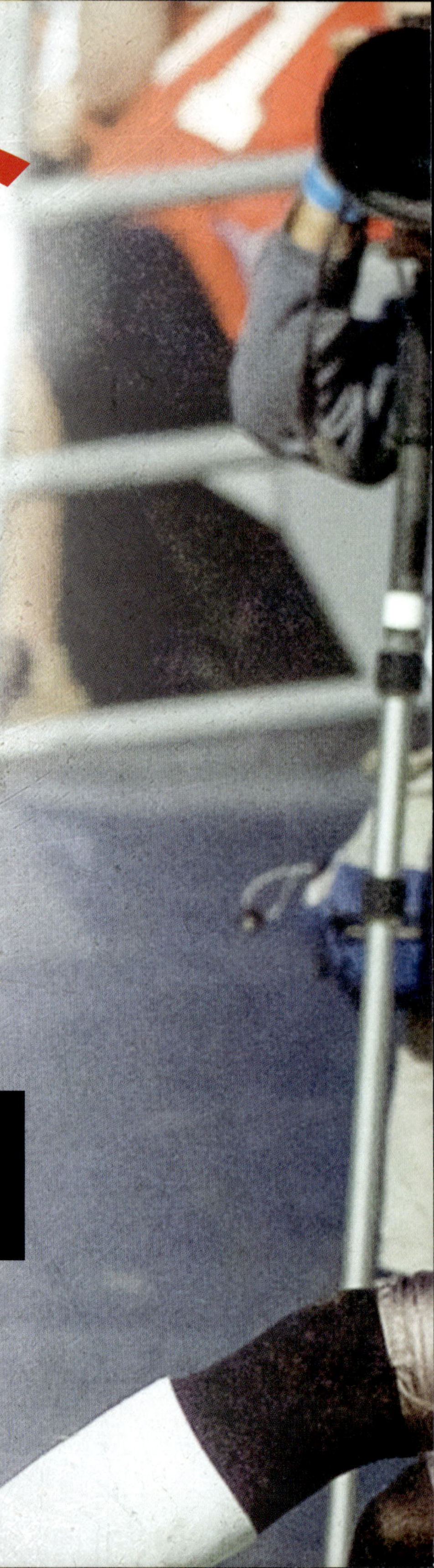

FAST FACT
Defensive back Ronde Barber played in his 225th game in 2012, the most in team history.

Gruden led the Bucs back to the playoffs two more times, mostly on the strength of their defense. But they never made it back to the big game. Key players from the Super Bowl team began to leave or retire by the mid-2000s. Gruden left after the 2008 season.

Ronde Barber intercepted 47 passes in his 16-year NFL career, which he spent entirely in Tampa Bay.

FAST FACT
Defensive tackle Warren Sapp was inducted into the Pro Football Hall of Fame in 2012. Derrick Brooks joined him the next year.

In 2015, Tampa Bay held the top pick in the NFL Draft. The Bucs selected quarterback Jameis Winston. Coupled with Pro Bowl running back Doug Martin, the Buccaneers may be at the start of their next great era.

Quarterback Jameis Winston once again has Bucs fans looking forward to the future.

TIMELINE

1976
The Buccaneers play their first NFL season, finishing 0-14.

1977
After 26 straight losses, the Buccaneers finally win a game, beating the New Orleans Saints 33-14.

1979
The Buccaneers win their first division title, make their first playoff appearance, and get their first playoff win.

1981
The Buccaneers win their second division title.

1995
Defensive end Lee Roy Selmon becomes the first Buccaneer inducted into the Pro Football Hall of Fame.

1997
The Buccaneers make their first playoff appearance in 15 years.

1998
Raymond James Stadium opens.

1999
The Buccaneers win their first division title in 18 years but lose to the St. Louis Rams in the conference championship.

2003
The Buccaneers defeat the Oakland Raiders to win their first Super Bowl.

2015
The Buccaneers select Jameis Winston with the first overall pick in the NFL Draft.

GLOSSARY

DEFENSIVE BACK
A player who tries to keep receivers from catching passes.

DIVISION
A group of teams that help form a league.

DRAFT
The process by which leagues determine which teams can sign new players coming into the league.

INTERCEPTION
When a defensive player catches a pass intended for an offensive player.

PLAYOFFS
A set of games after the regular season that decides which team will be the champion.

ROOKIE
A first-year player.

SACK
A tackle of the quarterback behind the line of scrimmage before he can pass the ball.

INDEX

Allen, James, 24
Alstott, Mike, 22

Barber, Ronde, 26
Bell, Ricky, 12
Brooks, Derrick, 6, 22, 29

Dilfer, Trent, 18, 19
Dungy, Tony, 19, 20, 21, 22, 25
Dunn, Warrick, 22, 23

Gannon, Rich, 6, 7
Gruden, Jon, 4, 5, 25-26

Jackson, Dexter, 6

Lynch, John, 6

Martin, Doug, 29
McKay, John, 13

Nickerson, Hardy, 19

Rice, Simeon, 7

Sapp, Warren, 22, 24, 29
Selmon, Lee Roy, 14
Spurrier, Steve, 8, 9

Testaverde, Vinny, 16, 17

Wilder, James, 16, 17
Williams, Doug, 10, 11, 12, 15
Winston, Jameis, 29

Young, Steve, 19

ABOUT THE AUTHOR

Todd Kortemeier has authored dozens of books for young people, primarily on sports topics. He is a graduate of the University of Minnesota's School of Journalism & Mass Communication and lives near Minneapolis with his wife.